ASI's WORLD RECORD

Written by Doug GeBraad   Illustrated by Scott Nash

Celebration Press
An Imprint of Pearson Learning

All morning long, Ashley's brother, Butch,
had been reading a book. He kept saying,
"Wow!" and "Cool!" as he read.

"What are you reading?" Ashley asked.

"Go away, pest," Butch answered.

As soon as Butch left for his piano lesson, Ashley ran to find the book. She couldn't read the second word of the title, so she took the book to her mother.

"What's this word, Mom?" Ashley asked.

"Guinness," her mother said. "That's *The Guinness Book of World Records.* It tells who's the best at different things. Who ran the fastest. Who danced the longest. Does Butch know you have his . . . ?" Ashley ran outside before her mother could finish the question.

Ashley went next door to find her friend
Tommy. He was a better reader than Ashley.
They sat beneath a tree and began to read
Butch's book.

"Look here!" Ashley cried. "This guy spit a
watermelon seed 68 feet!"

"How about this?" Tommy said. "Fourteen
kids leapfrogged 999 miles. It took them
ten days."

"I bet we could do it in eight days," Ashley said.

"No way," said Tommy.

"Oh, come on! We're good leapfroggers," Ashley said.

Ashley and Tommy leapfrogged twice around Tommy's yard before they collapsed into a tangled heap.

"I want my name in this book," Ashley said. "There must be something we're good at." Ashley turned to a page titled *Cats,* and slowly read, "The world's largest cat weighed 48 pounds." She looked at Tommy. "Are you thinking what I'm thinking?"

Ashley's mother was in the garden when Ashley and Tommy sneaked into the kitchen.

"Here, Tiger!" Ashley called softly, as she opened a can of tuna fish.

Tiger was used to only dry cat food and ate the tuna within seconds. Ashley gave Tiger a second, and then a third can of tuna fish. She couldn't find any more cans.

"Let's go get some more tuna from your house," Ashley said to Tommy.

When they returned to Ashley's house, her mother was holding Tiger in her lap. "Now, now," she said gently, "everything's going to be all right."

"Can we play with Tiger?" Ashley asked.

"I'm afraid Tiger's sick," her mother answered. "I don't know what she got into."

Ashley held two cans of tuna behind her
back. "Oh . . . well . . . gotta go . . .," she
told her mother.

"Bummer!" she said to Tommy when they were
outside. They went back to Butch's book.

9

"Skipping rope!" Ashley shouted. "What could be easier? This guy did 13,783 turns in an hour. We'll beat that. No sweat!"

Ashley quickly found her jump rope. "Tommy, you skip. I'll count," she said.

Tommy started real fast. Each time the rope went under his feet, Ashley shouted out a number. Tommy got to 43 jumps before the rope got tangled in his feet.

6, 37, 38, 39, 40.

"Try again," Ashley said.

Tommy kept skipping. Ashley kept counting. After ten minutes, Tommy was exhausted. "I couldn't jump 13,783 times in a year!" he panted.

"I don't believe that guy really did it," said Ashley.

"Look here," Ashley said. "This guy from Minnesota kissed 8,001 people."

"Yuck! Don't even think about it," replied Tommy.

"Listen to this one. 'A man from England ran 26 miles carrying an egg in a spoon,'" Ashley read. "We can top that. I'll be right back." Ashley went to get a carton of eggs and two spoons. She handed Tommy a spoon and placed an egg in it. Tommy took two

steps, and the egg fell and smashed onto the ground.

"This is hard," said Ashley, when her own egg fell and broke.

"All right, we'll start out real slow," Tommy said, as he carefully placed eggs in both their spoons.

One by one, all the eggs shattered on the ground.

When her mother called her for dinner,
Ashley was pouting.

"What's wrong?" her mother asked.

"We've been trying to set a world record," said
Ashley. "Tommy and I are just not good at
anything."

"You can't just get up one morning and set a
record," her mother said. "You need to

14

practice. Remember last year when Butch started playing the piano? He didn't even know which keys to use. Now he can play songs."

Ashley didn't like many of the songs Butch played. She hoped if she had practiced the piano for a whole year she would be better than Butch. But Ashley didn't say that to her mother.

The next morning, before Butch was awake, Ashley read the *Track and Field* chapter of his book. She chose the 100 meter run because it was the shortest distance. The world record was under eleven seconds . . .

Tommy came over and they measured 100 yards.

"Shouldn't we be measuring meters?"
Tommy asked.

"This will be close enough," Ashley answered.

Tommy used his stopwatch to time Ashley
as she ran. "A little over 40 seconds," he
called out.

For the rest of the summer, Ashley practiced running every day.

She ran in the early morning before it got hot (38 seconds).

She ran in the cool evenings, just before the sun went down (29 seconds).

She ran before lunch, when her stomach was empty (34 seconds).

18

Ashley ran
(27 seconds) . . .

and ran
(25 seconds) . . .

and ran
(22 seconds) . . .

By the end of the summer, Ashley's speed wasn't getting any faster.

"I'm no good," she complained to her mother. "I'll never set a world record."

"How long did it take you when you first tried?" her mother asked.

"Over 40 seconds," Ashley said.

"And how long does it take you now?" asked her mother.

"Twenty-one seconds," said Ashley.

"You've cut your time in half, Ashley!" said her mother. "When you return to school, your gym teacher can tell you how to run even faster."

Ashley went outside and ran some more.

Ashley kept running every morning.
When school started, she asked her gym
teacher for help.

"Sure. I'll be your coach," Ms. Farina said.
She taught Ashley the best way to breathe

while running. Then she showed Ashley the best way to move her arms.

Every day, Ashley got better and better. Soon she stopped thinking about setting a world record.

Ashley's World
Record

June 4	38 Seconds
June 28	34 Seconds
July 12	29 seconds
July 23	27 seconds
August 7	25 Seconds
August 15	22 Seconds

She was happy just trying to beat her own record.